Damaged Friends

Sad but true stories about damaged books

Lidia Vasquez

AuthorHouse™
1663 Liberty Drive
Bloomington, IN 47403
www.authorhouse.com
Phone: 833-262-8899

Because of the dynamic nature of the Internet, any web addresses or links contained in this book may have changed
since publication and may no longer be valid. The views expressed in this work are solely those of the author and do
not necessarily reflect the views of the publisher, and the publisher hereby disclaims any responsibility for them.

Any people depicted in stock imagery provided by Getty Images are models,
and such images are being used for illustrative purposes only.
Certain stock imagery © Getty Images.

This book is printed on acid-free paper.

ISBN: 978-1-4520-1548-4 (sc)

Library of Congress Control Number: 2010905989

Print information available on the last page.

Published by AuthorHouse 04/29/2022

authorHOUSE

At the start of every school year, Miss Lily, the librarian from Wilson School, goes to the back corner of the library, opens the file cabinet, and pulls out a small box labeled "Damaged Samples."

Miss Lily uses these books to show children
why it is so important to take care of books.
She tells the stories of seven books
that used to be checked out a lot
and how their lives were suddenly changed.
Would you like to hear the stories?

"Hi! I'm a book on poems about Valentine's Day.
I loved when that holiday was approaching
because I would always be checked out.
One day, I left the library with a sweet little girl."

"The little girl was reading me at home at her kitchen table while she was having a snack. I'm not sure what happened next, but all my pages ended up wet from soda. There was nothing Miss Lily could do."

"*Hola*, at least all your pages are still complete. I'm a Spanish language book about a little girl who wanted to get her long, long hair cut. I think my story was so good, that the little girl who had borrowed me wanted to try to cut something."

"All I know is that every page has been cut, and now nobody can read my story anymore. I wish the little girl wouldn't have done that."

"Greetings, I'm a book about one of the Presidents of the United States. Every year, I would get checked out when the children had to do a report on the Presidents. I especially loved teaching the children about James Buchanan because he is not as famous as some of the other Presidents."

"The boy who checked me out did do a report but also wanted to add extra things to get a better grade. Unfortunately, he could only think of adding things directly from me!"

"He cut the Presidential seal and a picture of James Buchanan right out of my pages. Now I can't teach anymore, and children are not going to know what important things he did for the country!"

"Hello, I was a really popular book. Every boy and girl knew the characters in my book because they were on a TV show. I was checked out so much that Miss Lily was always fixing me to make me last longer."

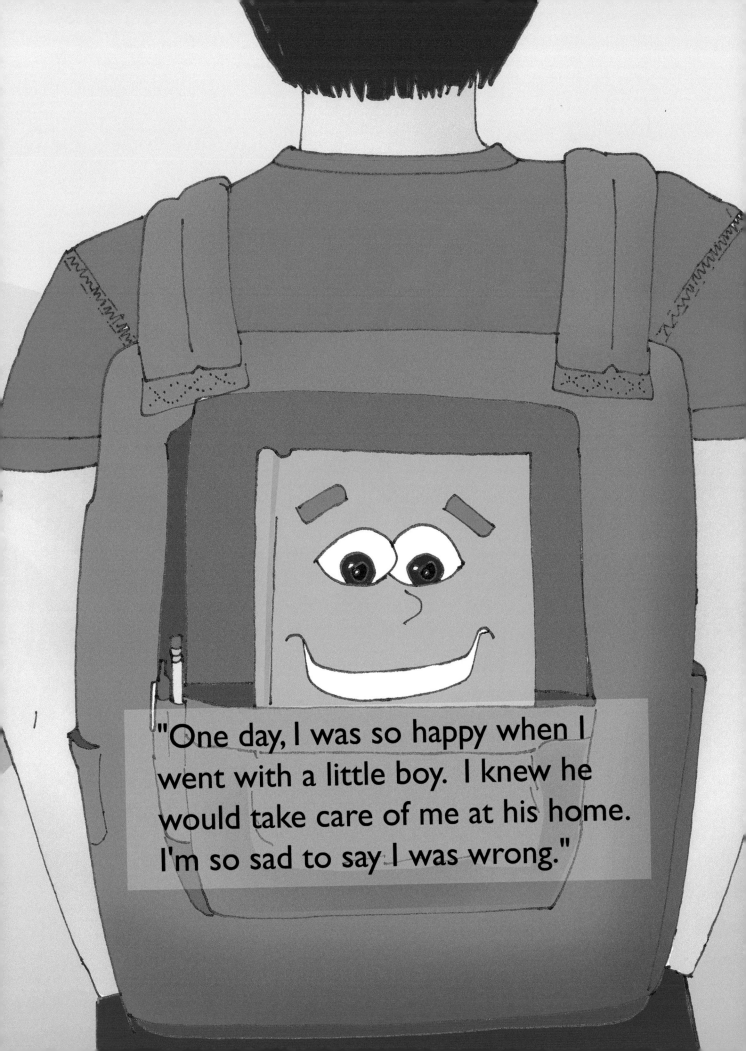

"His little brother loved coloring on everything, and when no one was looking, he grabbed me from the sofa and got his favorite color. Now, on every page, you will see blue all over."

"FILE" was the most public book. Because it was based on a famous movie, lots of people checked it out. All those fingerprints got all over the book as people turned its pages to remember the film.

"A little first grader wasn't supposed to take me home, but she did. At home, she wanted to add to the story and drew pictures with a pen all through the book. The pictures made me look very bad. Miss Lily could not put me on the shelf again."

"Hi, I'm an alphabet book. Parents would check me out to help their little ones learn the letters. The best part of the day was when I would hear little voices repeating the alphabet."

"The last time I was checked out, I was accidentally torn. Several pages were torn, and the mommy who had borrowed me got scared and tried to tape together the pages at home. She did not do a good job, because now I cannot be read."

"If she would only have told Miss Lily, I know Miss Lily could have put me back together so I could have been borrowed again."

"Hi, I'm a really funny chapter book. I remember hearing the boys and girls who would check me out always laughing. Those were some good times. Every time I tell my story, a tear runs down my face because I miss those days."

"The last little girl who borrowed me also checked
out another chapter book, but it was a serious one.
We were put in the backpack together. At first we
didn't get along, but just as we were enjoying each
other's company, my friend's life ended."

"The little girl put ice-cold bottled water in her backpack with us still in there. We both were soaked when we returned to the library. Miss Lily did her best to save my friend, but it was too late. My friend started getting black and fuzzy."

"Miss Lily had to throw him in the trash because he was not a healthy book anymore. I think I barely survived, but Miss Lily always checks me to see if there are any signs of fuzzy black stuff. I hope she never finds any, so I won't end up in the trash like my best friend."

After hearing these sad but true stories of how important it is to take care of books, Miss Lily reminds the children to not add any more books to this group. Please remember the stories, and always take good care of books.

Miss Lily puts the books back in the box. As she puts tape on the box, she hopes the children listened so she will not have to add another damaged book. Miss Lily sadly says goodbye to the books until the next school year.

Printed in the United States
by Baker & Taylor Publisher Services